Aging:
A Hairy Experience

Gerald Nilsson-Weiskott, Vincent Caputo, and Fred Juhl

Copyright © 2015 by Gerald Nilsson-Weiskott, Vincent Caputo, and Fred Juhl. 724903
Library of Congress Control Number: 2015916495

ISBN: Softcover 978-1-5144-1434-7
Hardcover 978-1-5144-1435-4
EBook 978-1-5144-1433-0

All rights reserved. No part of this book may be reproduced or transmitted in any form or by any means, electronic or mechanical, including photocopying, recording, or by any information storage and retrieval system, without permission in writing from the copyright owner.

Print information available on the last page

Rev. date: 10/19/2015

To order additional copies of this book, contact:
Xlibris
1-888-795-4274
www.Xlibris.com
Orders@Xlibris.com

Gerald Nilsson-Weiskott, Vincent Caputo, and Fred Juhl

This book is dedicated to all of us who are aging. We would rather choose this than the other option.

Acknowledgments

We could not do this without our friends and family, but particularly, thanks to Susan Nilsson-Weiskott, Peggy Caputo, and Terrie Juhl for their support and encouragement and for putting up with us for many years.

While this book is a parody on aging, we do not want to reinforce the negative stereotypes of the elderly. It is a chapter in our lives when we no longer need to prove ourselves and recreate who we are. It is a time to challenge our brains, keep active, and create a legacy for the next generation.

The Physical Changes We Endure

We have hair growing in places where we are not supposed to have hair and suffer the indignity of losing it where it used to be!

An ear hair comb-over

We've been "trumped."

Eyebrows keep on growing. Yeah! We can fly.

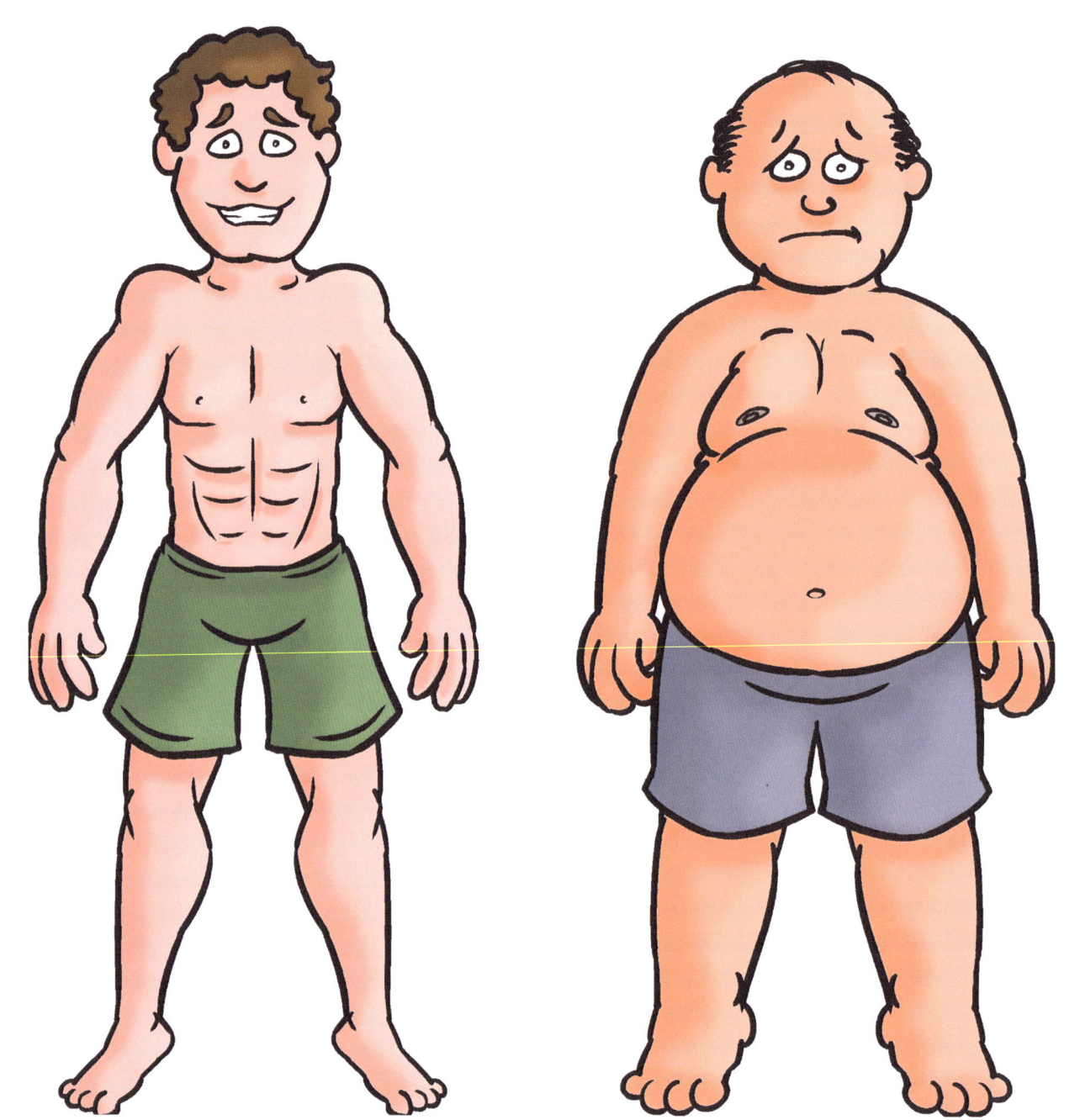

The transition over time from six-pack to keg.

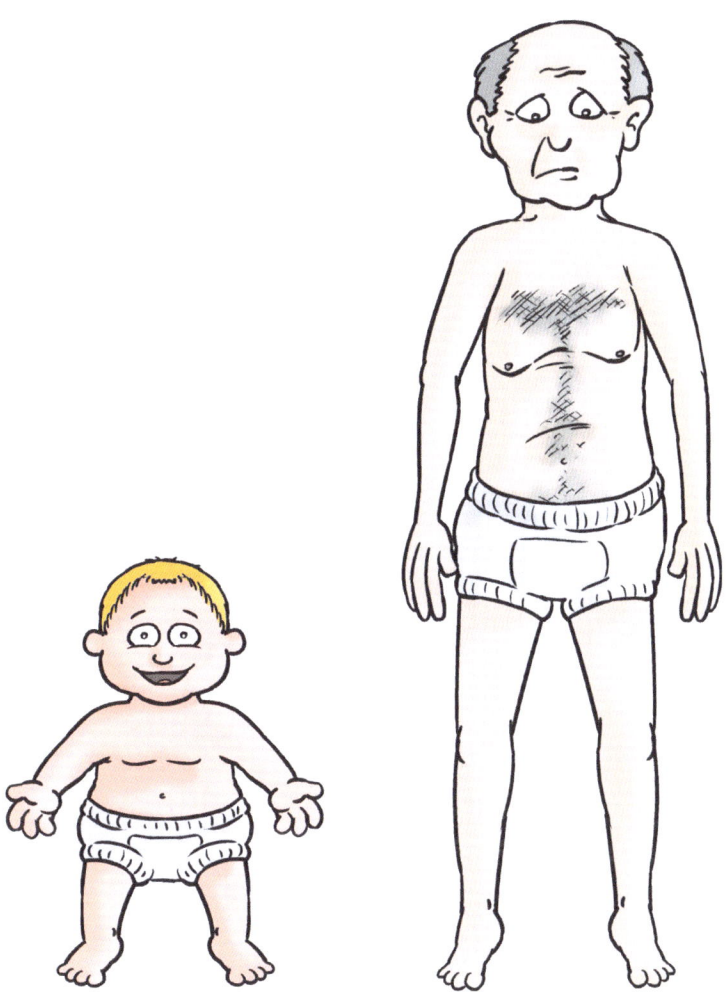

As we age, we revert back to childhood
I guess it "Depends" on how you look at it.

Once Again, the Similarity to Babies

The quest for pureed foods.

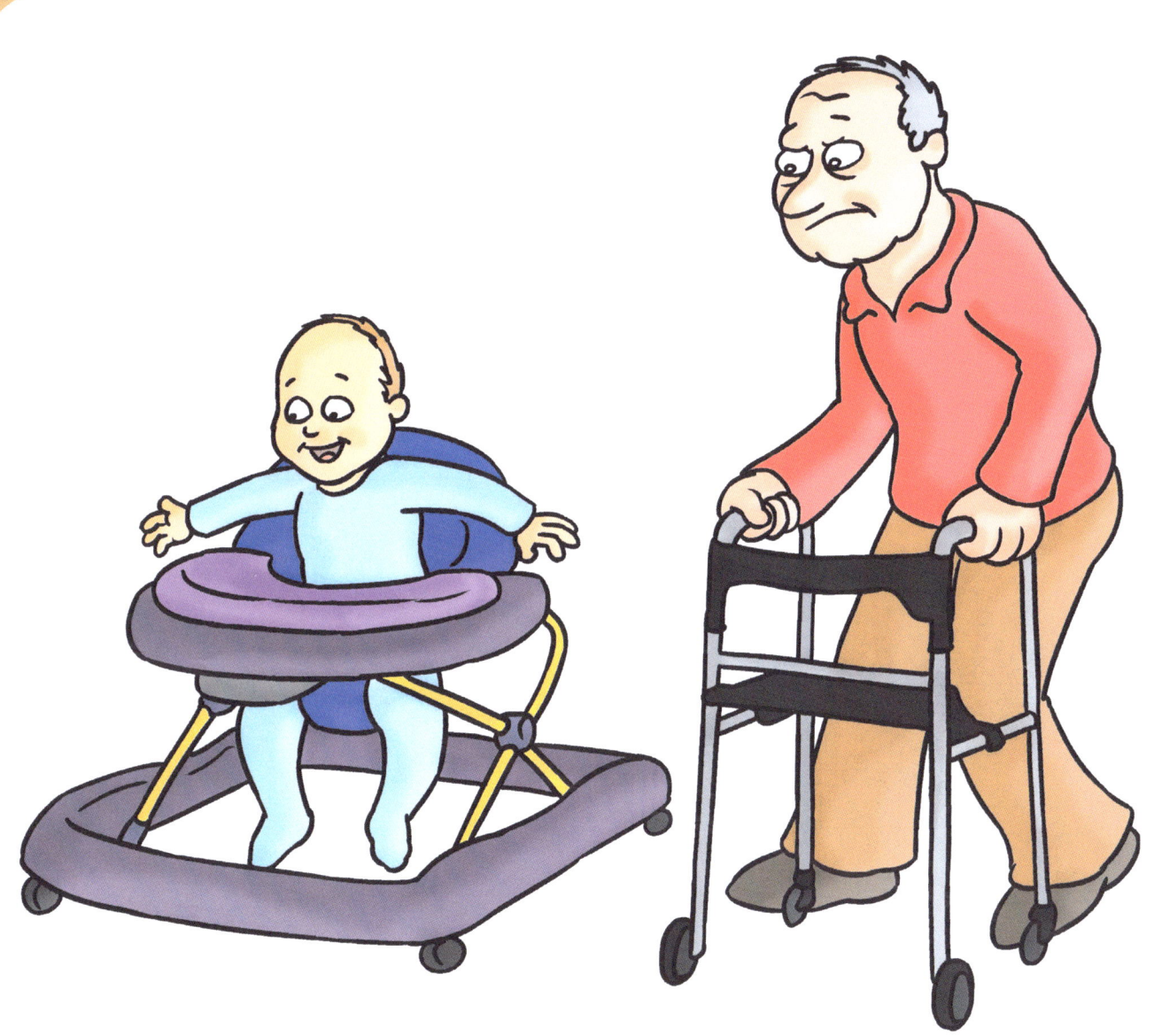

From Strollers to Walkers

Getting around town.

The Redistribution Paradigm

While the male butt gets smaller, the female butt gets larger.

Chinny Chin Chin

We do continue to grow, but necking becomes more difficult.

The Turkey Wattle

This is not something to give thanks for.

Gravity Takes Its Toll

I understand we wanted to keep abreast of things, but this is ridiculous.

Gravity Continued

Oh my god, I can't find my penis.

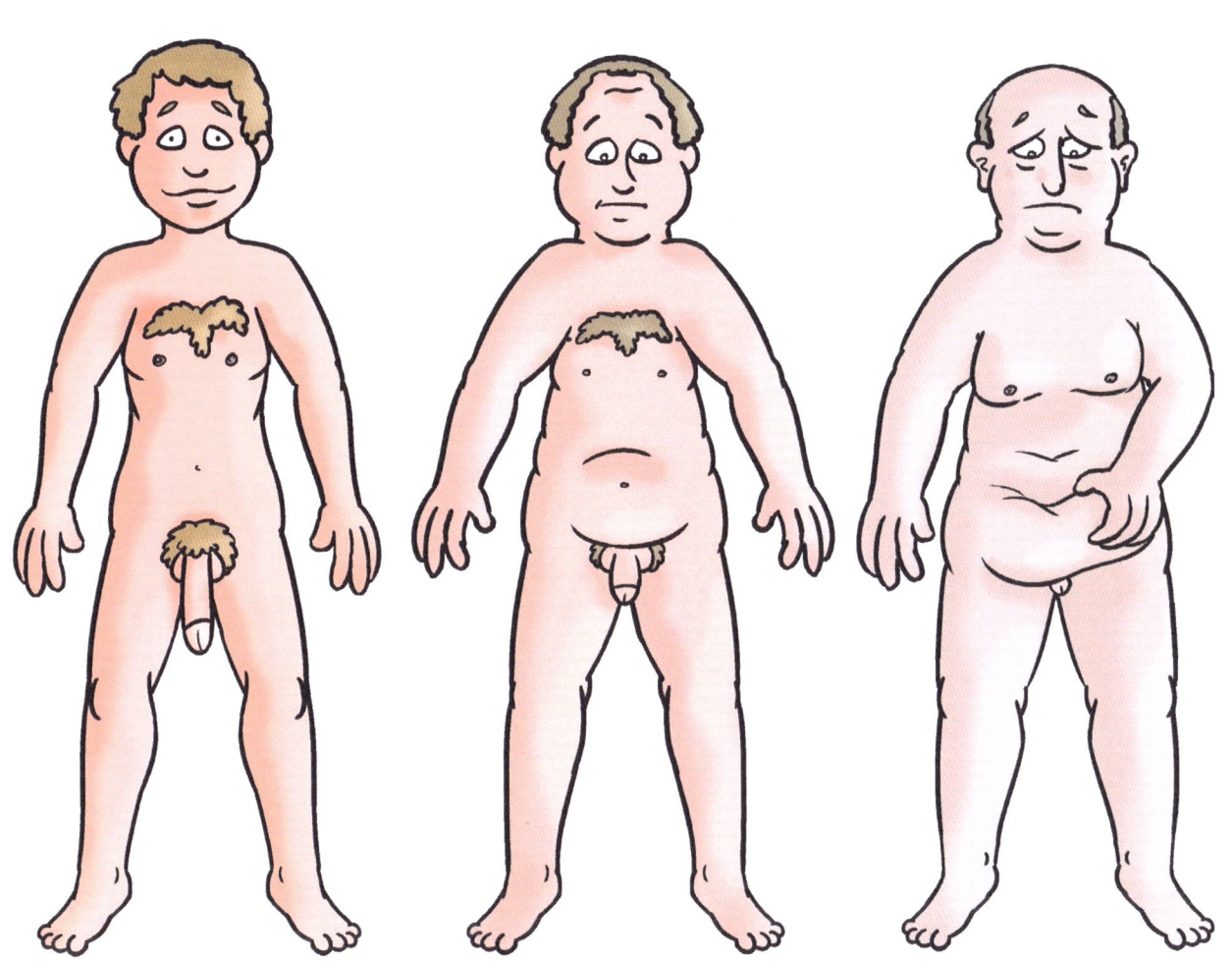

Why We Adopt Animals as We Age

Whoa! Did you just fart? What was that smell?

Traveling Becomes More Difficult

From pillbox to suitcase.

Sex and Aging

Welcome to sex without partners. We've really got to hand it to this guy.

Just trying to cop a feel.

From Counting Sheep to Counting Floaters
No, not those kinds of floaters.

My god, what was I thinking? Now I'm going through the alphabet, from A to Z, trying to figure out my nephew's name.

Watching the Pawn Stars reruns does remind us that cognitive functioning is somewhat impaired. The good news is we keep laughing at the same jokes!

I used to pride myself on having a good sense of direction. Now I have none (direction).

Our social network has expanded. Unfortunately, our best friends now include the social security administrator, our health professionals, and the funeral director.

Competition used to be on the athletic field. Now winning is that our names are not in the obituary column!

Boy, we're excited that if this book is a success, we might be on the *Letterman Show*.

About the Authors

Gerald Nilsson-Weiskott is a retired psychologist, previously from Brooklyn, New York, and then Ohio, where he was the director of training for the Ohio State University Counseling and Consultation Service. He was the president of the Leadership Development Group, where he focused on human resource development, organizational consultation, and executive coaching. He is known for his humor, which is helping him design the next chapter of his life, where he is often found cooking, hiking, listening to music, and traveling. He received his PhD from the University of Texas and currently resides in Lago Vista, Texas.

Vincent Caputo grew up in Salt Lake City, Utah, and Council Bluffs, Iowa. He graduated from Buena Vista University with a BA in business management. He worked for thirty years in the manufacturing industry in the field of material management until retiring in 1999. He enjoys the earth sciences, weather spotting, volunteer firefighting, and coffee in the morning with the "walking group." He currently resides in Big Lake, Missouri. In 2007, he debuted in the Bad Boyz of Big Lake calendar, where he was strategically clothed as Mr. October.

Fred Juhl was born in Northwest Iowa and grew up on a farm. He relocated to Omaha while in the Air Force and currently resides in Papillion, Nebraska. He graduated from the University of Nebraska in Omaha and has worked in IT at Mutual of Omaha for the past thirty-three years. He is a founding member of the band Spectacle, which was inducted into Iowa's Rock and Roll Hall of Fame in 2002. His passions include being with his family, following the University of Nebraska sports, and riding his Harley Classic.

About the Illustrator

Simon Goodway is a freelance artist living in the UK. After working for a few years as a software engineer, he switched to illustrating full-time in 2005 and hasn't looked back since. He has illustrated children's books, greeting cards, corporate logos, and all manner of things, from skateboards to magic tricks.

For volume 2 suggestions, contact the authors at agingahairyexp@gmail.com.

Printed in Great Britain
by Amazon